Sleepless Nights

Arisha Jahawir

BookLeaf
Publishing

India | USA | UK

Presentation by *BookLeaf Publishing*

Web: www.bookleafpub.com

E-mail: info@bookleafpub.com

ISBN: 9789357446877

First edition 2022

DEDICATION

For my past, present and future selves. Go slow but steady.

On the sleepless nights in which you wrote these, you wrote so it would quiet the noise in your head.

On the off chance that someone else might read these, you only hope it can engage their thoughts, if only for a fraction of a second.

For they are not a reflection of who you are, only where your mind has ventured.

To: YOU

To my dearest,
What you mean to me you will never understand
The moments shared,
The moments yet to be shared.
One day.

One day,
I will hold your hands
Because I know you get shy
When someone reaches out to hold
Your hands.

Your hands,
To me, seem like a treasure.
Masterpieces, they have composed
Your tears, they have wiped:
My hands.

My hands,
Are the only thing they have yet to hold.
I can feel your touch,
Even though I don't know your touch.
Do you know?

Do you know?

I want to see your shy smile,
As I reach out to hold your hands.
I want to comfort you
Make you feel at ease.

Make you feel at ease,
Fingers interlocked,
As you squeeze my hands
To reassure,
Both you and I.

Both you and I
That I am your Solace
And you are my Home.
I am your desire
You are my desired.

You are my desired,
To be loved by you
I can think of no drug,
More potent
My Undoing.

My Undoing,
Would be finding you.
No.
You finding me,
For I know you.

For I know you,
But you, not me.
You know not,
That I want to trace
You-r

You-r,
Pretty veins that line
Your blessed hands
Veins that ultimately reach
Your heart

Your heart,
Pure yet damaged,
Tormented
Because you know there is something:
Missing from you.

Missing from you,
Is me.
You don't know me.
But I know you
I know you.

I know you,
Star,
Cloaked,
Let me uncover you.
My dearest love.

Release ME.

What is there to live for?
Will it all matter in the end?
Who will remember us?
10 years after? 5 years after? 1 year after?
7 months after? 2 months after? Days later?
Or only on the anniversary of our death, one day
per year?
Should they be burdened to remember us?
Do they owe us?
Do we owe them?
Have you earned the right to be remembered?

Were you kind?
Were you helpful?
Were you understanding?
Were you patient?
Did you listen?
Did you sacrifice?
Did you suffer?
If so, then you've loved.

But were you loved?

I want to be remembered.
I want to be loved.

I crave release from this endless cycle.
Let me ride on into the sunset
Or in to the brazen hellfire
For judgement is what I live in and judgement is
what awaits me still,
What is there to live for?

In my Mind, There Exists

It takes me so long to make up my mind
Even though I know what I want

I still struggle with making a decision
I consider everything

Doubt
You're not ready

Failure
You're not good enough.

Regret
Why don't their dreams align with the dreams I
dream for myself?

Disappointment
Is that your inevitable destination?

Denial
There is still enough time, the world is waiting
for you.

Desire

To live hand in hand with you even though I do
not deserve you

Shame
There is someone out there who has worked
harder than me

Realization
I deserve everything I aspire

Determination
I will show them

But then,
What if?....

And so,
The cycle continues.

Act I

[[Are you still working?
…

Yeah. I'll be done in a few mins
Okay.

Sleep if you're tired.

I'll wake you up anyways :P
:') I know. I'll wait

Ok. Be there soon.

I'm coming]]

The sight of her dances in my eyes.
The first time I saw her
A velvet trail hung from her shoulders
Following her closely
Adorned with pearls and sequins
Silver dangled from her ears
And seemed as if they blinded my eyes
As I caught a glimpse
of the most perfectly flawed profile
The bridge of her perky nose

Raised, yet sparkling with the diamond that
permanently adorns it.

From stealing glances to
Having my glances returned
Glances becoming gazes
Morning texts,
Evening calls,
And suddenly ,
My last, first date.
She held my hands "You are more than a friend
to me"
My lover
Felt unlike anything I had ever felt before.

My inspiration
My comfort

She keeps me going,
The only one that can stop me.
She will take me in her arms
Everything will vanish.

She is so many things
To me,
For me,
Within me.
She is waiting for me.

Act II

I take him in my arms,
Everything vanishes
It feels like
the first time I saw him,
Every time I see him.
His hair carefully slicked back
Exposing his beautifully broad forehead
with just enough strands falling down
As if they wanted to touch those
Phoenix eyes.
I turned abruptly
Before they could glance upon me.
From the corner of my own eyes,
I felt his harrowing gaze.
The gold threadwork on his black robe
Commanded the attention of all.
Yet, he seemed bothered by
A sequined velvet trail.

I look up at him
Tonight, his forehead is fully covered
with his messy hair.
I know right away he's had
A tempestuous day.
His kisses land on my

Cheek,
Neck,
Lips,
And before he rests his head on my chest,
As always,
He pecks my nose.
A habit that remains a mystery to me.

And Beyond

How vast the world must be
To say it has 7 wonders is a check

What about those we can't see
We are but a speck

What lies beyond us
Will we ever know

Always seem to be making a fuss
Humanity has become a show

The insignificance of our lives
Is nothing but motivation

From where the arrogance derives
It must be hallucination

What is yet to come
Reward for our sins

What will we become
Birds without wings

Flightless
Trapped

13

The story of humans, Timeless
Adapt

(Un)Breakable

How come when you're miles away
I feel closer to you than when
You are within my reach.

I only have to reach out
Attain your touch on my fingertips,
Your taste on my lips,
Your aroma intoxicates my every sense.

Yet i cannot reach you
Unattainable,
So the closer you are is the farther you are

Miles away from me,
I imagine that you are close
I console myself
Distance is the reason you won't have me in
your arms tonight.

Within my grasp,
My heart struggles to console itself
That we are improbable

Improbable, because while my heart falters
My mind cannot rationalize

The possibility of impossible
 For my soul will forever be unaccompanied.

Heart, mind and soul
The existence of my being
Craves you for who you are.

Selfishness will not allow me
To wish for your heart
To seek comfort in another
While I serve mine on a platter

Left unattended
Untouched, untasted,
Yet carved into little pieces

Blood curdled and dripping
Waiting for you to taste
So that I may intoxicate your every sense
The way you have, me.

I Want to Live

The biggest dream they sell you
is also the biggest lie they tell you
Go to college
Invest in an education
Your life will be set after that
You will have a path to follow
You will discover yourself
Who you are, what you like
Where am I now?
Where are you now?
Behind the closed doors of Privilege
And Experience
That you never planned to open for me
You sold your pipe dream
The only door open
Is the one into my deposit
I owe you what I do not have
You sold me hope
Promised me security
Painted on canvas, my future
Presented it to me on a 8.5x11 sheet coated in
blood, sweat, tears
Downwards is the slope

Insecurity haunts me hand in hand with
obscurity
My dreams I am left to suture

Don't get me wrong
I am not mad at education
Acquiring knowledge is life's biggest investment
They say as you sow you shall reap
I am empowered
I can think for myself
I know justice from tradition
I am bold enough to ask questions
Isn't that what you wanted?
Me to think for myself
Why are you agitated?
Perhaps because the turn around
Is me posing the questions to you
Did you think you would be exempt
You call me ungrateful, disrespectful
I now see the truth for what it is painful,
disgraceful
I have it easy, you say
"Back in my days"
My favorite phrase of pretense.
You are the sunset,
I am the dawn of the new day
But I am trapped in the dark of the night
Restrained from shining my light
You call me lazy

You call me rebel
For trying to forge new paths
In truth, you feel threatened
I forge a new road,
Yours become obsolete
Maybe you'll say this doesn't qualify
There is no rhyme
There is no scheme
You are lost in time
I want to break out of the regime
How do I iambic my feelings
How do I flow and cadence my anger
You want me to follow your rules
Set me free.

I want to live.

Defib

They wanted everything from life
They had it all planned out
their future,
the future:
their life.
Everything they ever wanted,
Everything they thought they needed
I was sure, so they were sure.
With every beat
I pumped excitement, joy, hope,
love
Every surreptitious meeting
I skip a beat.
Have you ever felt
terrified and at peace
all at the same time?
Have you ever given yourself wholly and
completely?

Have you ever been lured into a
false promise of
Excitement, joy, hope,
love.
Rashly, quickly, surely
I led them astray.

Their pain is incomparable to the guilt
that is mine
Irrational, deceitful, misleading, stupid fool
Less and less
reliable every day.

They have turned against me
they no longer come to me,
listen to me
They no longer trust me.
I have been tamed,
replaced
by my longtime rival
Rationality.
Never sure, always questioning
damned logic
I am reduced to a muscle,
Veins, vessels, capillaries.
Main function: Pump blood.

But what about them?
How do you rationalize
hope, joy, excitement, love?
Maybe I can win them back...?
Should I win them back?

Requite

Everybody sees the way you look at me now
But nobody sees what it's doing to me
All they have from me are expectations
A burden so great
Everything between us goes uprooted

How do I tell you of the way you terrify me
Terrify me, that we would lose the love between
us
Why is it only valid if its romance
What about the promise of friendship you made
Why am I being punished for the promise you
broke

I cannot lose you
You cannot gain me
The vacuum between us
Starts to fill with resentment
Why have you done this to us

I wish there was a way to make you understand
The pain you have inflicted
How can I,

All the great works composed by men
postulating unrequited love,
So few consider the torment of the object of
those affections.

Act III

Home:
The place where one lives permanently
Subdued in love
Tamed by loss
Embroiled with passion
Yet resisting, with hardship
Every union reminds
Of The Loss
And so bodies engulfed
in the flames of agony
whose relief is each other
Lie side by side
Filled with dreams
Wishing, the space between them
Was filled by the Angel
The universe stole back
Just as quickly as it gave them

"I love you."
The words shake the velveteen bedchamber
Silence
Doubt resonates one side
Anger permeates on the other
"Why?"
A question directed at the heart

"Why?"
A question asked back
This time with infinite meanings
Why would you ask that
Why do you doubt me
Why wouldn't I
Why do you tear my heart
Why why why why why
In the end,
No answer is given
Only confirmation
When bodies revel in each other
Entangled twisted inseparable:
Home.

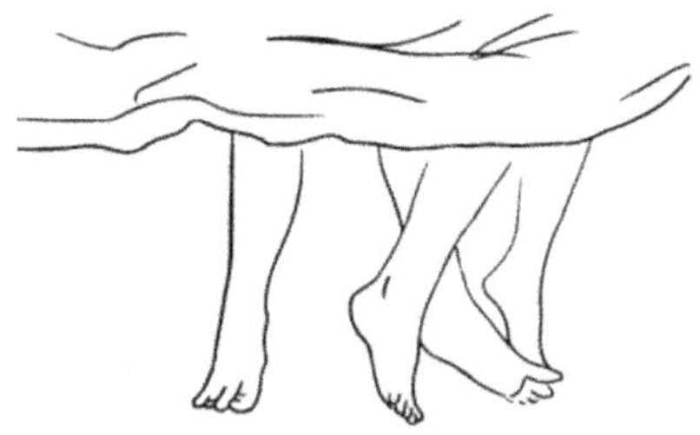

What do you Cost?

Sacrifice your dreams
In service of money
Immolate your passion
In service of money
What makes the world go around
If not money

Born into it
Earn it
Chase it
Scam it
Damn your soul
In the service of money

Those who have it
Try to tell you it isn't everything
Is that right?
Then why don't you give to
Those who need it,
Serve money

We, all of us, brought to our knees
In the service of paper
The true universal language
Translates every where

By the click of a button
In service of money

Lives can be destroyed
Lives have been destroyed
Lives will be destroyed
Where next will the
Currency of life take us
In service of money.

Vacuum

Satiate the hunger
From within
In these troubling times
Too much is given up on
At the same time
So much is taken on
Still, it feels empty within
Do this, Do that
Try this, Try that
Don't do that, Don't try that
The within is full
Yet empty
Missing something
Guilt pervades when
Realization hits
Compared to others
The plights (within) are miniscule
For a minute, gratitude rear its head
Until it's meaningless again
The empty within never leaves
You alone

It's Okay

I just want you to know
It's okay.

That job you didn't get
That frustration you feel
That raise you want to ask for
Go ahead and do it
Because
Está bien.

That jealousy you feel
That subsequent guilt
That self doubt you grapple with
It's human
And
C'est bon.

That outfit you can't afford
That shame you feel
That dream of better days
Will come to pass
In the meantime,
Theek hai.

That lover that didn't call you back

That anger you feel
That is a sign
It's time to move on
In the end,
Gwaenchanhayo.

That thing you did that one time
That embarrassment you still feel
That is remembered by no one but you
Do yourself a favor
At last, forget about it
Méiguānxi.

That annoying thing you hear
That things happen for a reason
That question that bugs you, WHY ME?
The truth is though, the future is unknown
With this in mind, trust that
It's okay.

Musings for a Muse

The voice that resonates
through speakers
Vibrates the barriers
of Space
to reach my ears
Only then do I understand
what Music is meant
To Be.

How can I relate
to Someone
I don't know
Someone, not Something
because I feel you
Through your words
The wings on your back
become Mine.

Borders, Barriers
Torn, Shattered
To reach me
All I have to do
is close my eyes.
Even now as I
put pencil to paper

Chaos fills my head.

My desire to vociferate
Is both inspired and
Quelled by you
Who knows rebellion.
Your caterwauls
Turned into art
by Passion,
Raw talent.

The power of you
Is such that
Your genius meets millions
Yet, somehow
Customized to my heart
Does that make me insane
Or is that your intention
To invade me

The way your voice does
The first time,
I heard its depth
I wasn't looking for
The low vibrations
Reeling me in
I have been on hook
ever since
Unable to escape.

Tormented by (your) existence
Taunted by (my) insignificance
To repay you
Though nothing is owed
How come
You're the only one who hears
Every time I plead
Please save my life.

Act IV (Epilogue)

Her hair, smells like summer tonight
His hand, rests on the nape of my neck, delight

Her smile, gleams with a hint of sorrow
His worry carried between his brows, furrow

Her gaze, avoids mine, control
His stares, pierce through what should be my
soul

Her heart, belongs to me
His questions, unwavering, plea

Her body, fits mine, the lost piece of the puzzle
His touch, trailing down to caress, jolts me,
subtle

Her attention, finally mine, salvation
His breath, reeks of adoration

Her cheeks, flush as she allows me to look upon
her, sublime
His mind, put at ease as I devote to him, my time

Her lips, curve as she watches me work
His mind, so brilliant, jerk

Her approval my endeavoring, I dare
His heart and soul, laid bare

Her understanding, aligns with my mind
His persona, unlays in my lap, no longer
confined

Her ugly side, I have the pleasure of knowing
His beautiful heart, I covet, ever glowing

Her love, renders me devout
His drunken stupor, also seeks me out

Her scolding, like the sweet taste of wine
His peace of mind, with mine, intertwine

Her days, ends with me
His days, begins with me

For if she ever leaves
For if he ever leaves

Her --------
His --------

The One I wrote in College / Sonnet 031

His smile stops me in my tracks
His eyes give me hope
Into my heart he hacks
I feel like I'm under the influence of dope
My lover, a man beyond compare
His body sculpts under my fingers
How did I get into this illicit affair
The sense of his touch lingers
If love feels like heaven, then love is he
Bless me with him in every life
Fair Aphrodite! this is my plea
He hopes to one day call me wife
    Yet, by the devil, I cannot trust
    Tis' just lust waiting to combust.

Silk Cotton

Trudging thru
The snow battling the grips
On the outsole of my boots
The fresh grass of the past
Springs to mind.

Dew drops still sparkling
As you walk around the yard
Brushing your teeth
Picking half-blossomed hibiscus
To offer with morning prayers
The sun already scorching
as if it's high noon
Setting out for school
Barely at the end of the street
Sweat beads already gathered on your nose.
The shout of your niece
Captures your attention
Running around, pampers lagging behind
Playing at 7:45 am
Oh! To be a toddler again
Where the day consists of: play + eat
Not: quadratic equation + instant headache
The commute to school

A bus, a boat across a whole river, and another
bus.
Still somehow less harrowing than waking up
On a winter's morning
The salty waters of the Demerara river
Splashes on your uniform as you take in the
scene of the Stabroek tower
Perhaps the only angle
Where the capital looks to be at peace.

Morning fatigue halts abruptly
As some gather on the corridor
Catching up on the latest gossip
Others bustling to copy homework
Before the morning bell
Rings us into the system.
The afternoon bell doesn't ring soon enough
So the gossip can continue
Who said what today in class
What pair was spotted under the steps at lunch
Which teacher was made to reconsider their
career choice today,
The whole spill.
The thrills of the afternoon session
Draws to a halt
At 4pm.
The rules are clear
Be back home before it's dark out.
This afternoon the street

looks different than this morning
The sides lined with cows and horses
after a day of grazing
Terrified of the cows,
Zig-zagging thru the street to avoid them
Yet, a fondness exists
Those very cows provide a glass of milk
Every morning.
The orange of the setting sun
Shadowed by the mango tree in a
Neighbor's yard. Your eyes set upon
the about to be speckled ones
It won't be long now
While the tree might be in one yard
The unwritten village rules says,
The fruits reaped belong to everyone.

The taste of mangoes jolts you back
As the bitter taste of coffee hits,
Fuel, so you can last the rest of the day
Hot coffee, milk, two sugars,
Burn the tongue and warms the insides as it goes
down
And all you wish is for it to be

The incomparable juice of the
Buxton Spice, rolling down your hands
As you bite into its soft, stringy flesh

The mango, the rest of the mangoes around the
world wish it were.

Something tugs on your skirt
It's your niece, fresh as a daisy
Powder patted across her neck
Smelling like she should be on a Johnson &
Johnson advert
You lift her up and she plays with the knot
on your loosened tie.
You ask her if she wants to wear it someday
The pride you feel when she nods
You're the first in your family to wear this
uniform
And you hope you won't be the last

As the flurries hit your nose
Whilst you trot down the avenues
You remind yourself it's all
"For a better life"
How foolish to think that is what we all seek
When we've already lived
The best days of our lives.
You take comfort in knowing
Your niece is now growing
And hopefully living the best days of her life.

Driven

Tormented by thoughts driven by anxiety
Loneliness exacerbates the torment
Driven by the anxiety of
"Will it forever be like this?"

Tormented by anxiety driven by thoughts
Hidden in the identity of woman
Burdened by the identity of woman
"Will it break me or will I break it?"

Tormented by thoughts of the past
She carries the scars of a tragedy she doesn't
remember
Feels like the body of a stranger
"Will it become you or will you become it?"

Tormented by anxieties of the future
The coming of who I am meant to be
Feels too far for my taste, yet I can catch a whiff
of its aroma
"Will it come to pass or will it pass me?"

US

What would your love feel like?

Would it burn me up or

Would it stifle me till I can no longer breathe?

Can I bask in the embers

Or would you have me

Gasp at the indignations?

Perhaps it's a feeling I cannot yet imagine

A thought I have yet to think of

Pangs yet to be discovered.

Body and soul,

I want to know.

Heart and head,

I need to know.

I sometimes wonder if any of the things I
imagine will ring true?

No need for words,

Glances would relay thoughts

Glares would end fights

Gazes would inquire forfeit.

Suturing pain and desire

Creating an entity that heals

You and I.

A haphazard attempt to erase the past,

Building a future that's worth

You and me.

Divided, lost

United, found

Us.

You and I.

You and me.

US.

Always you with different versions of me.

I cannot change who I am

But I can be who you need me to be.

Friend, lover, fighter

Source, inspiration, critic

Desire, weakness

Haven, strength

Will you be to me what I am ready to be for you?

Perhaps you would take me as I am

Would you make me,

Or leave me in a rubble

How could I recover from the familiarity of you

Is it possible to convalesce from a fulfilled desire?

Everything seems to be a question

I have no answers since

I do not yet have you.

To know that I am willing to make myself

Weak

Not to be with you

But with you,

A sure sign of damnation.

Passion ablaze like hellfire

Tender as doves but

Engulfed with predatory desire

Hunt and capture until

Submissive.

Rally in fervor,

Pleasured in unison.

Can Our inception mirror that dream I once
conjured?

I never thought I'd be your choice,

So, I ran not brave enough to endure

Rejection from you.

Except you came for me,

Not to tell me

I love you.

But: Please love me,

You begged.

I somehow knew I was in a dream,

Yet I held you with reassurance

In this dream and the daydream that is life,

All you have to do is find me,

And I will keep you.

Waited

I wait for something that I don't know

What then am I waiting for?

What is it that I anticipate with desperation?

That, someday, somehow I will be happy?

Because I deserve it?

That all the fantasies that play out in my head

will manifest

The lights will shine on me

The world will welcome me with open arms

I will earn a spot

Riches, Respect

Honor, Loyalty

It seems that I only want to take

Is that selfish, when I feel like I've only been

giving?

Confidence, Hope

Peace of mind, Self-doubt

Isn't it time I was given something in return?

Give and I will give back

Because I understand what obscurity feels like,

I promise to pull you out of the abyss

On a journey with me to
Identity, Security
Dignity, Friendship

Or maybe it is You I wait for
The you that will make me,
 Us.
Together, fighting against the world
Fighting because nothing good ever comes easy
Fighting because you; we are worth it.
We
Defenseless, naked
Protected, shielded
Against the world
Against each other
Gaining strength from our biggest weakness:
"You"
The building blocks that were made to fit into
each other
Make me whole, complete
Render me with meaning
Give me
Love, Legacy

Glory, Security

As I will unhesitatingly and undoubtedly,

Take you;

Take me

Let me love you, please you, serve you, inspire

you

Take my pieces,

Puzzle them with your own

Our cracks and crevices merged

As we create the whole picture

That has been missing since the dawn of our

time.

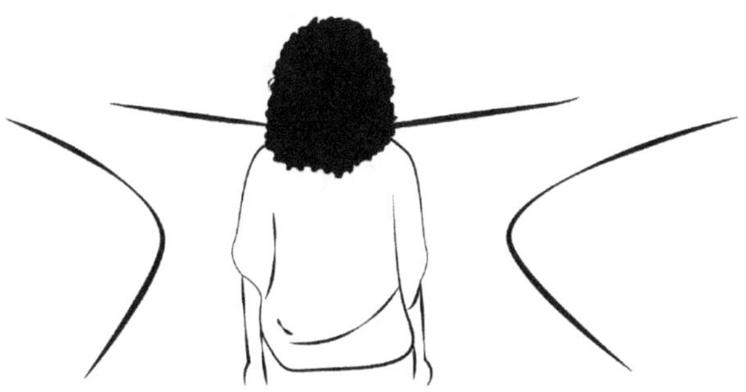

> "Two roads diverged in a wood, and I ---
> I took the one less traveled by,"
>
> -Robert Frost.

9 789357 446877